D1272778

Toriyama Sensei gave me some pointers on how to bow correctly.

I'm talking about how to draw someone bowing!! (LOL)

—Toyotarou, 2019

Toyotarou

Toyotarou created the manga adaptation for the *Dragon Ball Z* anime's 2015 film, *Dragon Ball Z: Resurrection F*. He is also the author of the spin-off series *Dragon Ball Heroes: Victory Mission*, which debuted in *V-Jump* in Japan in November 2012.

Akira Toriyama

Renowned worldwide for his playful, innovative storytelling and humorous, distinctive art style, Akira Toriyama burst onto the manga scene in 1980 with the wildly popular *Dr. Slump*. His hit series *Dragon Ball* (published in the U.S. as *Dragon Ball* and *Dragon Ball Z*) ran from 1984 to 1995 in Shueisha's *Weekly Shonen Jump* magazine. He is also known for his design work on video games such as *Dragon Quest*, *Chrono Trigger*, *Tobal No. 1* and *Blue Dragon*. His recent manga works include *COWA!*, *Kajika*, *Sand Land*, *Neko Majin*, *Jaco the Galactic Patrolman* and a children's book, *Toccio the Angel*. He lives with his family in Japan.

SHONEN JUMP Manga Edition

STORY BY **Akira Toriyama**
ART BY **Toyotarou**

TRANSLATION **Caleb Cook**
LETTERING **Brandon Bovia**
DESIGN **Joy Zhang**
EDITOR **Marlene First**

DRAGON BALL SUPER © 2015 BY BIRD STUDIO, Toyotarou
All rights reserved. First published in Japan in 2015 by SHUEISHA Inc., Tokyo.
English translation rights arranged by SHUEISHA Inc.

The stories, characters and incidents mentioned in this publication are entirely fictional.

No portion of this book may be reproduced or transmitted in any form or by any means without written permission from the copyright holders.

Printed in the U.S.A.

Published by VIZ Media, LLC
P.O. Box 77010
San Francisco, CA 94107

10 9 8 7 6 5 4 3 2 1
First printing, December 2020

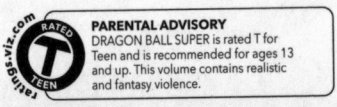

STORY BY
Akira Toriyama

ART BY
Toyotarou

CAST OF CHARACTERS

STORY THUS FAR

A long, long time ago, Son Goku left on a journey in search of the legendary Dragon Balls—a set of seven balls that, when gathered, would summon the dragon Shenlong to grant any wish. After a great adventure, he collects them all. Later, he becomes the apprentice of Kame-Sen'nin, fights a number of vicious enemies, defeats the great Majin Boo and restores peace on Earth. Some time passes, and then Lord Beerus, the God of Destruction, suddenly awakens and sets out in search of the Super Saiyan God. Goku, by becoming the Super Saiyan God, manages to stop Beerus from destroying the Earth and starts training under him with Vegeta. Then, our heroes travel to the future to fight Goku Black and Zamas of the parallel world. Soon after, the Lords of Everything decide to host a Tournament of Power featuring the strongest warriors from twelve universes. After some time, the ancient villain Moro escapes from the Galactic Prison and travels to New Namek in search of the Dragon Balls. Goku and Vegeta confront him, but are unable to prevent him from making his wishes. Moro's ability to absorb life energy seems like too much to handle, but now, Goku, Vegeta and the Great Lord of Lords slumbering inside Boo are off to confront Moro again!!

CHAPTER 49 **Outer Space Battle** 07

CHAPTER 50 **Great Escape** 53

CHAPTER 51 **To Each Their Own Plans** 99

CHAPTER 52 **Goku and Vegeta's Training** 145

DRAGON BALL SUPER

CHAPTER 49: OUTER SPACE BATTLE

WE NEED TO GET OFF THE PLANET NOW!!
OUR ENERGY WILL BE ABSORBED BY MORO TOO IF WE STAY MUCH LONGER!
RRMMMM
AKRAK
!
THIS WHOLE SPECTACLE MUST BE KINDA HARD FOR YOU TO WATCH.
ROMISED THEM I'D SURVIVE EVEN IF I WAS THE ONLY ONE LEFT.
...
NO WONDER I'M OUT OF BREATH-- IT'S THE ENERGY DRAIN!!
HUFF!
TMP TMP TMP
BW OO M

THEN LET'S ALL SURVIVE AND REBUILD A PEACEFUL NAMEK! AND THAT MEANS DEFEATING MORO FIRST.
GOTCHA!
MAYBE HE FORESAW HIS OWN DOOM AND ENTRUSTED THE FATE OF OUR PEOPLE TO ME. THAT'S WHY IT'S MY RESPONSIBILITY TO SURVIVE THIS.
THE GREAT ELDER NAMED ME HIS SUCCESSOR BEFORE DISASTER STRUCK.
HE DID?
THE VILLAIN SHOULD BE UP AHEAD ONWARD
WMP
WMP
WMP
WMP

HRAH!!
VOOM
VOOM
FSH
ZOOM
RAHHH!!

SHP
FWS
FWAH
WHA THE-?!
OVER THERE !!
WHRL
ZOOSH

NOT SO FAST !!
FWSH
TCH!
WHFF
SHP
WHFF
FSH
FWAHH

SOME-THING SEEMS OFF!
HIS REAL BODY ISN'T HERE...
W-WHAT GOIN ON?
WHERE IS HE ABSORB-ING THE PLANET'S ENERGY FROM?!
CRAF WHER HE GC
WMP WMP WMP WMP
GRP
O-OVE THERE

WAIT, KAKARROT !!
ZOOSH
SKWEEZ
SAIYANS CAN'T SURVIVE IN THE ACUUM OF SPACE!!
THAT'S OUTER SPACE!
UGH!
I'LL GO.
OH RIGHT ...
!
ZOOSH

NOM
BWAK

AH!
YOU DARE TO WEAR THAT DETESTABLE FACE IN MY PRESENCE?
GREAT LORD OF LORDS?
GRR!!
GRP
FWP
KAPOW
POW
!!
WHAM

KA
SLAM
SHP
WHFF
ZOOM
ACK!
ZOOSH

!!
FSHH
DARN IT. THEY'RE OUT OF SIGHT!!
DAMMIT... THERE'S NO WAY TO TELL HOW THE BATTLE IS GOING!!
AGENT MERUS! MORO AND THE GREAT LORD OF LORDS HAVE LEFT NAMEK'S ORBIT.
PERHAPS THE FIGHT HAS BEGUN ?!
NAMEK'S NOT LOSING ENERGY ANYMORE.
FIRST, WE ATTEND TO GOKU AND VEGETA!
GOKU AND VEGETA REMAIN IN THE ATMOSPHERE. WHICH PARTY SHOULD WE GO AFTER THEM?

ZOOM
PEW
PEW
PEW
PEW
BOOM
BOOM
BOOM
BOOM
ZOOSH

TAKE THIS!!
SHOOM
GAH!
BWOOMP
!!
SHWIP
TMP

GWAH
GULP
SHOOM
HE GOT ME!!

WHAM
SLAM
SM

HFF!
HFF!
...BUT NOW THAT MY POWER EXCEEDS YOURS, THEY NO LONGER TROUBLE ME.
HMF
I WAS CONFUSED BY YOUR STRANGE POWERS...
!
BECAUSE THIS IS UN-IMPRES-SIVE.
DID SOMETHING HAPPEN TO YOU THESE PAST TEN MILLION YEARS?
RESIST AND I'LL SEAL OFF YOUR MAGIC AGAIN!
LISTEN, MORO-- YOU'RE GOING TO COME QUIETLY BACK TO GALACTIC PRISON.
!
GRP

GO AHEAD. DO YOUR WORST.
THE OLD SEALING TECH-NIQUE, IS IT?
HEH HEH ...
...
...
...
NO, I THOUGHT NOT. I DON'T SENSE THE SAME GOD POWER YOU ONCE HELD.
OU'RE HARP.
...
I DARE-SAY YOU LACK THE POWER TO UNLEASH THE SEALING SPELL, RIGHT?

AT THIS RATE, HE'LL BE TOO MUCH FOR US TO HANDLE SOON!
AND WHAT ABOUT THAT MAGIC SEALING TECH-NIQUE?
HOW INFURI-ATING.
H-HEY... DID YOU JUST FEEL MORO GETTING EVEN STRONGER ?!
COME ABOARD.
GOKU, VEGETA.
ZOOSH

WHAT DO YOU MEAN?!
IN FACT, I SUSPECT THAT AS HE IS NOW, THE GREAT LORD OF LORDS CAN'T EXECUTE THE KAI KAI-MATORU.
NO...
I GUESS HE CAN'T SHOOT OFF THE SEALING MOVE UNLESS MORO'S BEING HELD IN PLACE?
W-WAIT, WASN'T THAT OUR ACE IN THE HOLE?!
IT OCCURRED TO ME EARLIER WHEN BOO ATTEMPTED TO USE IT.
.BECAUSE OF THE SPLITTING THAT BOO NDERWENT.
IT'S MOST LIKELY...
INDEED IT WAS ...
EXPLAIN YOURSELF.
THAT PINK GUY'S KINDA CREEPY. ONE TIME I EVEN AW HIM SPROUT EXTRA ARMS FROM HIS BODY...
YES...
YOU MEAN THE SPLIT BETWEEN HIS GOOD AND EVIL HALVES?
WHAT CAN'T THAT WEIRDO DO?
HE SPLIT ?!

SO THE GOD POWER WAS PASSED ON TO THE EVIL HALF OF BOO?
I SUSPECT SO.
MORE FUSING, HUH? LOTTA THAT GOING AROUND ...
HUH? SERIOUSLY?
AND WHILE WE CAN'T SPLIT, WE CAN ASSIMILATE.
WELL, MY PEOPLE CAN REGROW LOST LIMBS.
THAT LITTLE GUY HAD ACTUAL GOD POWER IN HIM?
TCH...
BECAUSE THE GOOD BOO INHERITED THE GREAT LORD OF LORDS'S PHYSICAL APPEARANCE, I ASSUMED HE RECEIVED THE GOD POWER AS WELL BUT MAYBE THAT POWER WENT TO THE EVIL BOO INSTEAD.

GAH...
ZOOM
SH
OOM
FSH
PO
W

KRSHH
KRSHH
KRAK
DID SOMEONE STEAL YOUR POWER...
...AND REDUCE YOU TO THAT PINK, PIGGISH FORM FROM EARLIER?
FLIP
DAMN
WHAT

GAHHH!!
KR SH
UGH ...

I SEE.
WHEN HE WAS OBLITERATED, SO WAS MY POWER...

...!

HOW WONDERFUL IT IS NOT TO HAVE TO FEAR THAT ANYMORE.

...IT'S CLEAR TO ME THAT NO BEING IN THIS UNIVERSE POSSESSES THE POWER TO SEAL AWAY MY MAGIC.

NOW THAT I'VE TAKEN A GLIMPSE AT THOSE LATENT MEMORIES...

GIMMICKY TECHNIQUES LIKE THAT NEVER ACTUALLY GET THE JOB DONE.
IT WAS ALWAYS GOING TO TAKE BRUTE FORCE TO BRING DOWN THIS FOE.
I THINK VEGETA'S RIGHT...
MORO! DEAD AHEAD!
...WHICH IS WHY WE GOTTA DO SOMETHING NOW.
DAMMIT... WE'RE COMPLETELY POWERLESS IN OUTER SPACE!
BOOM
RRMMM

GOKU! VEGETA!
YEP.
NATURALLY. MAGIC ASIDE, WE ARE THE STRONGER GHTERS. JUST ONE OF US AT ULL POWER IN SUPER SAIYAN BLUE FORM OULD HANDLE HIM.
ARE YOU ABSOLUTELY CERTAIN THAT THE TWO OF YOU ARE MORE POWERFUL THAN MORO?
ROGER THAT.
IN THAT CASE, I WILL DRAG MORO BACK TO THE SURFACE OF PLANET NAMEK, WHERE YOU TWO CAN FINISH THE JOB.
BWOOMP
KLK
?

ZOOM
I'M OFF.
IS THAT ONE OF THEM SPACE SUITS?
PLEAS RETUR TO NAME IN THE MEAN TIME
BWOOOM
HEF!
HEF!
CAN ALL YOUR OUTFITS DO THAT?
NAH, THAT ONE WAS CUSTOM-MADE FOR MERUS.
CAN'T. WON'T. I'M WAY SCARED OF OUTER SPACE, MAN.
SO YOU'RE NOT BACKING HIM UP, JACO?

VO
OM
FWIP
GWORMP

TUG
YANK
SWING

WHRRL
SNAP
ZOO SH

GRAP
ZOOM
TMP
ZOOM
I CAN'T WIN ALONE.
YES, OF COURSE.
WE NEED TO GET MORO BACK TO NAMEK SOMEHOW SO THAT THE TEAM CAN BATTLE HIM TOGETHER!
TH-THANK YOU.
ARE YOU STILL WIT US, GREA LORD O LORDS!

BEFORE THAT, CAN I CONFIRM SOMETHING WITH YOU?
CAN YOU STILL USE INSTANT TELEPORTATION?
YOU KNOW YOUR STUFF.
AS A LORD OF LORDS, YES, I CAN.
EXCELLENT. WHEN THE TIME COMES...
SLAM
SHP
YOU AGAIN !!
BLASTED GALACTIC PATROL!!

PEW
FWSH
BOOM
PEWPEWPEW
YOU
COM
AT M
WITH
TOY

FWSH FWSH FWSH
OM
OM
OM
FWSH FWSH FWSH
PEW PEW PEW
CEASE THIS FUTILE FARCE.
TCH!
...
FWSH FWSH FWSH
PEW PEW PEW

...THAT'S ENOUGH!!
SHOOM
I SAID
FWP
ZOOSH
BOOM

GRRK
TUG
KRAK
ZOOM

SMASH

C-CURSE YOU!
M-MY EYES!!
TMP
GRP
!
I'VE GOT YOU NOW!

LET'S GO AFTER HIM, VEGETA!!
I'M SENSING MORO'S CHI BACK ON NAMEK NOW!
AH!
!
SPOT ON!
FWP
THANKS A LOT, MERUS!

FSH
WE'RE AT FULL POWER NOW, SO YOU WON'T GET AWAY AGAIN.
MORO! READY FOR A FAIR FIGHT?
...

WE MUST HURRY BACK TO NAMEK TOO.
YOU WERE AWESOME OUT THERE, MERUS!
WOOM
BEEP
YES, I GUESS SO.
CUZ, Y'KNOW, THEY'RE A TEENY TINY BIT STRONGER THAN ME.
THOSE TWO WILL HAVE THAT GUY BEAT BEFORE WE KNOW IT.
IT STILL HOLDS ENERGY? WHAT A WASTE TO LEAVE FOOD ON MY PLATE.
AH, PLANET NAMEK ...

HEH HEH...
...
WE'RE ABOUT TO DESTROY YOU ONCE AND FOR ALL!
I DON'T THINK YOU COMPRE-HEND THE SITUATION
THE THIRD WISH!
?
SO FOOL-ISH. SO NAIVE.
HA HA HA
YOU SEEM TO HAVE FORGOTTEN SOMETHING QUITE IMPORTANT.
!

DRAGON BALL SUPER

CHAPTER 50: GREAT ESCAPE

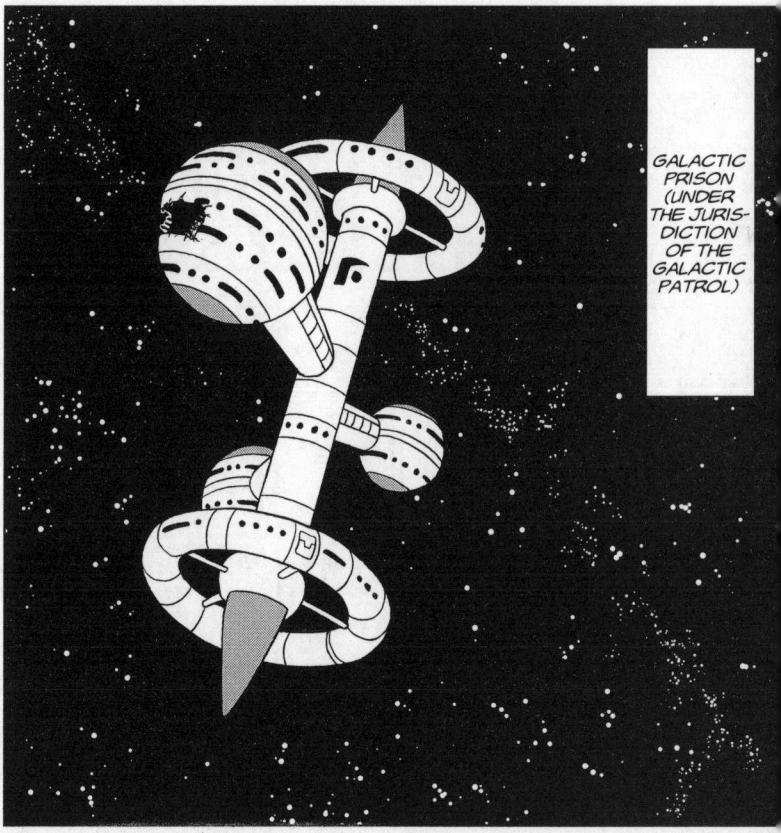

HE
LTED
THE
ARS...
THAT MORO GUY'S MAGIC IS SCARY. IT EVEN GOT HIM OUT OF THIS PRISON!
KLNK
YEAH, SINCE CAPTAIN MERUS SET OUT TO RECAPTURE MORO, WE GOTTA HAVE THINGS IN TIP-TOP SHAPE ON OUR END.
AND THE GALACTIC KING WANTS THIS REPAIRED QUICKLY? THAT'S A TALL ORDER...
NAH, MORO'S THE ONE TO WATCH OUT FOR. THE OTHERS COULD NEVER ESCAPE ON THEIR OWN.
MAYBE WE SHOULD BE WARY OF THE OTHER PRISONERS HERE INSTEAD.
NO CLUE. BUT FOR NOW, WE JUST GOTTA BELIEVE IN THE GALACTIC PATROL.
BUT MORO WAS ALREADY ABLE TO BREAK THROUGH THE PRISON'S SUPERSTRONG DEFENSES. WHAT'LL STOP HIM FROM DOING THAT AGAIN?
TMPTMP

BAM
TMPTMP
WHRR

SHWP
SHWP
GET IN!
VWOOM
KCHK

HOW MANY TIMES DO WE GOTTA LOCK YOU THREE UP? CAN'T YOU LEARN YOUR LESSON FOR ONCE?
THEY MUST ACTUALLY LOVE IT IN HERE.
FREAKING UNBELIEV-ABLE.
KCHK
TCH...
WOOM
A LIFE OF CRIME'S THE ONLY KIND FOR US.
HMP
ZOOM
GLOW
NEW NAMEK

ZOOOM
GLINT
KA
ZAM
HUH? WHAT'S HAPPENING?!
KZZT KZZT
!
?
KZZT KZZT

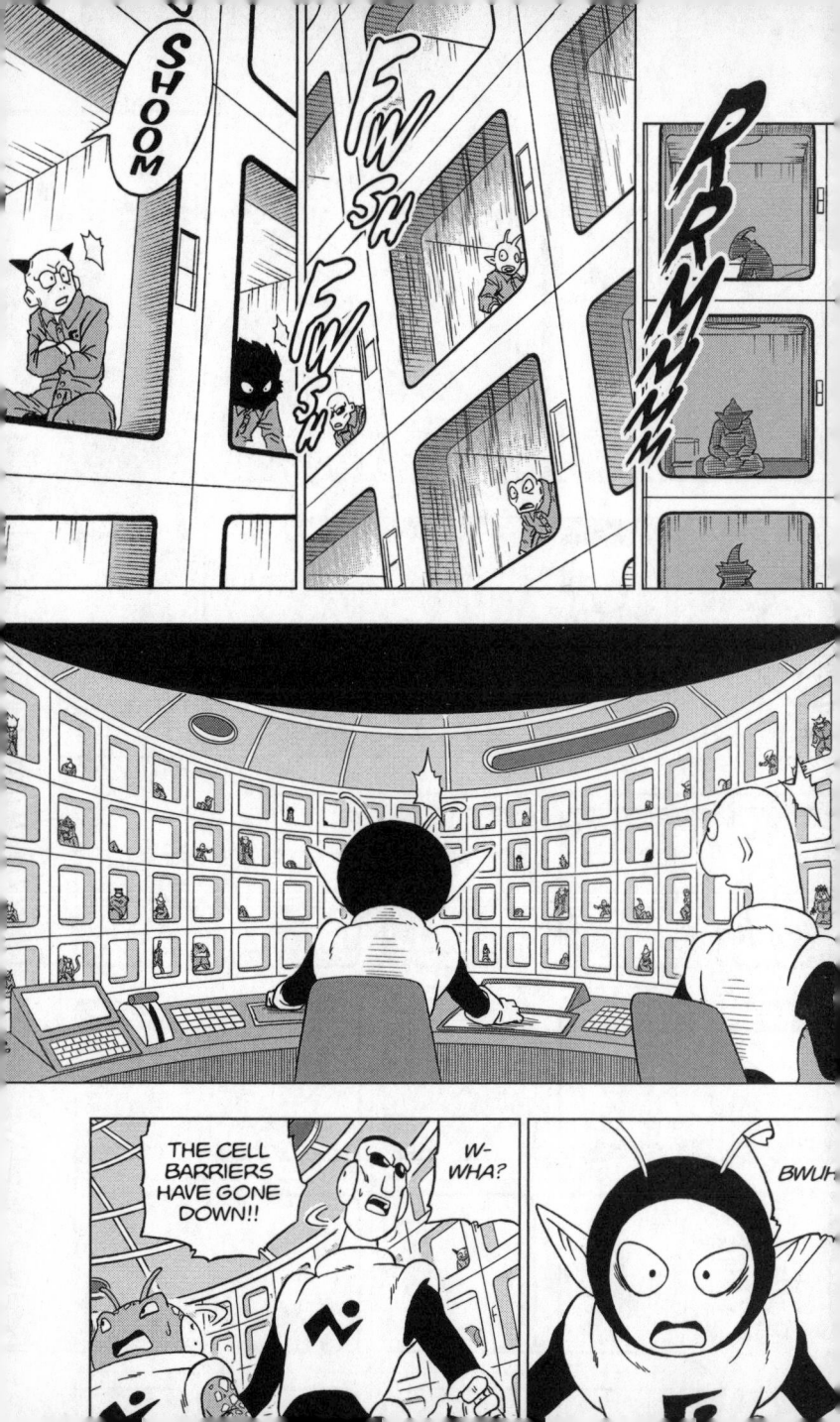
SHOOM
FWSH
FWSH
RRUUUU
THE CELL BARRIERS HAVE GONE DOWN!!
W-WHA?
BWUH-

ERE'S NO RRIER!
OOH...
HIT THE SWITCH, QUICK!!
WAS THERE A MAL-FUNC-TION ?!
R-RIGHT.
HOW'S THAT POS-SIBLE?!
THE POWER'S OUT!
THIS IS BAD!
CHK CHK
CHK CHK
THE BARRIERS ARE DOWN!
MTTR MTTR
IS THIS OUR CHANCE TO MAKE A BREAK FOR IT?!
MTTR MTTR

...LORD MORO.
YOU REALLY PULLED IT OFF...
YEAH WE'RE FREE
TIME TO RUN!
...
I'M GUESSING THIS IS MORO'S DOING?
B-BIG BRO, THIS'S OUR CHANCE TO RUN TOO!
YO, SAGAN-BO.

TOMP
WHAT THE HECK'S GOING ON?!
SHOOT, I CAN'T GET AHOLD OF GALACTIC PATROL HQ!
B-BACK IN YOUR CELLS, INMATES!!
WHAT DO YOU THINK YOU'RE DOING?!
AH... AHH.
Y-YIKES !!

FLK
ACK!
GRP
!!!
TOMP

KNOW OUR SPACESHIP'S HERE, SO YOU'RE GONNA HAND IT OVER, 'KAY?
W-WHAT ABOUT US, BIG BRO?
!
...
WE AIN'T GONNA HURT YA.
THE REST OF YOU ARE COMING ALONG TOO!
T'S OIN HE RTY.
THIS COULD GET FUN...

BEEP BEEP BEEP
IN-INCOM-ING!
O-OH NO...
WHAT'S THE SITUA-TION?!
THERE'S A EMERGEN DISPATCH STRAIGHT FROM HQ
WHAT?! WHAT HAP-PENED?
SAY WHAT ?!
...HAVE STAGED A MASSIVE PRISON BREAK!
THE INMATE AT THE GALACT PRISON

I'M EMEM-ERING...
AH... AHH...
ONE MENT AGO? THAT WAS RIGHT ABOUT WHEN MORO MADE HIS WISH, RIGHT?!
YES, THE MESSAGE CAME LATE BECAUSE WE LOST CONTACT WITH THE PRISON...
AND THE INCIDENT ACTUALLY OCCURRED ONE MENT AGO.
IN THAT CASE...
O-OH YEAH. THEY BRAIN-WASHED YOU AND FORCED YOU TO STATE THEIR WISHES, RIGHT?
YES...
HMM? REMEM-BERING WHAT?
THE FINAL ONE!
MORO'S WISH...
...THAT EVERY PRISONER IN THE GALACTIC PRISON GO FREE.
YES, FOR THAT FINAL WISH, I DEMANDED ...

?
L-LOOK, VEGETA! UP THERE!!
HERE THEY COME.
YOU LE THEM LOOSE BUT WHY?!
HEH HEH ...
SHOOO
SHOOO
SHOOO

A SPACE-SHIP?! IS IT THEM...?!
I'M FEELING A LOT OF CHI SIGNA-TURES IN THERE!!
NRRRM
BWO OM
LOOK OUT!!
!!

SKOM
GRAP
YOU THINK IT'S THE FREED PRISONERS?!
A SURPRISE ATTACK?!
SKFFF
RRUMMM

AT YOUR SERVICE, LORD MORO.
RRMMMM
AS ROMISED, I WILL HARE MY POWER WITH ALL OF YOU.
WELL DONE INDEED, SAGAN-BO.
YOU'VE BROUGHT A SMALL ARMY, I SEE.
HE MUST'VE BEEN WAITING FOR HIS PALS TO SHOW UP!
TCH... MORO'S UP THERE NOW!

HUH?
!
BWOOM
THE ONES INSIDE... I JUST FELT THEIR CHI GROW!
I THINK MORO MUST'VE USED HIS MAGIC AGAIN!
SHP
SHP
SHP
SHP
WHRRR
TOMP
TOMP

ARRRGH!!
WE HAD NO IDEA HE'D BE BRINGING FRIENDS...
SO THIS IS WHY HE SEEMED SO CONFIDENT.
...MY CON-VICTS.
HAVE AT THEM ...

GWOOOO
ON YOUR TOES! THESE GUYS SEEM TOUGH!!
UGH!
SHOOM
SHOOM
WHEEF
TAP

WHFF WHFF
WHAM
ZOOM
GRAP
GRAP
WHRRL
SLAM

GUH!
GAHH!
WHAM
WHAM
WHAM
HAHH!
!
UGH!
KRAK
KAWHAM

BOOM
GAHH!!
FLIK
Ew Ew Ew Ew
RMMBL

HOW'RE THEY THIS STRONG?!
W-WHOA, THESE AIN'T YOUR EVERYDAY GALACTIC PATROL GUYS!
...
SO GO! THEY CAN'T HOLD YOU ALL OFF AT ONCE.
UNLESS YOU WANNA HEAD BACK TO THE SLAMMER, YOU'D BETTER OBEY LORD MORO'S COMMANDS!
KEEP GOING AT 'EM!
HEY! DON'T TURN YELLOW ON ME

POW POW POW
ZOOOM
BWOOM
HUH?
GOD FORM ?!
HUH?
BWOOM
MORO'S STARTED ABSORBING ENERGY AGAIN!!

I'LL HANDLE HIM.
N-NOT SO FAST!!
TMP
TMP
WOOM

SLAM
KR
AK
GWAHH ...
HMPH!
WOOM
UH?
WHAP
PICK YOUR-SELF UP, KAKAR-ROT!

SKFF
THE MOMENT WE DROP OUR GUARD, OUR TRANSFORMATIONS FAIL US!
SHOOM
TCH!
SHOOM
YOU OKAY, BOO?!
UGHH ...
SKF SKF
SLAM
WHAM
DARN ...
THAT BATTLE AGAINST MORO IN SPACE EARLIER MUST HAVE TAKEN A TOLL ON HIM.

POW POW POW
KA WHAM WHAM
WHAM
WHAM

TO CREATE AN IDEAL GALAXY WHERE I AM FREE TO CONSUME PLANETS AS I WISH.
GATHERING THESE ALLIES IS ONE SMALL STEP TOWARD THAT END.

WHAT'RE YOU REALLY AFTER HERE?
WHAT'S THE POINT OF ALL THIS?

H-HEY !!
MO-RO !!

...I DETEST THE SORT OF PEACE THAT YOU PEOPLE SEEK TO PRESERVE ON THIS PLANET AND OTHERS.
WHAT I CAN SAY IS...
DO YOU HOLD A GRUDGE AGAINST THE GALACTIC PATROL THEN?
I WON-DER.
...SHOULD BE ERADI-CATED.
ALL WHO WOULD STRIVE FOR SUCH NON-SENSE...
WOOM
WOOM
UGH
THAT JERK!

AMMIT! HOW MANY TIMES ILL WE FALL OR HIS TRICKS ?!
AND NOW WE CAN'T EVEN GO SUPER SAIYAN...
ZOOM
WHAM
WHAM
BY VE," OU EAN ME OO?
HUH?
I CAN HELP AS WELL!
I...
WE HAVE TO HELP OUR ALLIES, AGENT JACO!
THE CON-VICTS HAVE ALL GATH-ERED HERE!
OH NO!

I CAN'T FIGHT, BUT AT LEAST I CAN HEAL YOUR INJURIES
ZAP
ZAP ZAP
ZAP
THUD THUD
MORO MUST ONLY BE ABSORBING ENERGY FROM US!
BLAST! THESE FOOL AREN'T GETTING AN WEAKER...
TMP
TMP

PEW PEW PEW
PEW PEW PEW
MERUS! JACO!
!
PEW
PEW PEW
AS THINGS ARE, WE'VE NO CHANCE OF DEFEATING MORO! WE MUST RETREAT!!
PEW PEW PEW
BLINK
WAKE UP!
P-PLEASE ...

HRM? WHO'RE THEY?
THEY HAVE BACKUP OF THEIR OWN?
CHAK
NO!!
PEW

AT THIS ANGE ?
W- WHAT THE HECK?
LING
SO GRAB MY HAND! WE'LL ESCAPE WITH INSTANT ELEPORTA-TION!
I HEAR YA, MERUS.
R- RIGHT.
HEY! YOUR NAME'S IRICO, RIGHT? YOU GOTTA TAKE THE SHIP AND GET OUTTA HERE!
USE YOUR OWN INSTANT ELEPORTATION TO WARP TO GALACTIC PATROL HQ! PLEASE!
GREAT LORD OF LORDS!

FWP
WE'LL MEET AT YOUR HQ.
VER WEL
...
GRAB ON TO ME, AGENT MERUS
YOU TOO, VEGETA!
WHAT'S THE HOLD-UP?
IF HE ABSORBS ANY MORE ENERGY, I WON'T BE ABLE TO USE INSTANT TELEPORTATION AGAIN!
STUPID GOD POWER...
STUPID MAGIC SPELLS.

...?
PEW PEW PEW
PEW PEW PEW
AND YET, I'VE BEEN REDUCED TO THIS!!
WE SAIYANS PRIDE OURSELVES ON OUR PHYSICAL MIGHT. A WARRIOR RACE HAS NO NEED FOR FANCY PARLOR TRICKS!!
FORGET INSTANT TELEPORTATION!!
LET'S GO! YOU WANNA DIE HERE OR SOMETHING?!
HEY!
WHAP
ACK!
ZOOM

GO AHEAD, KAKAR-ROT.
WHOOPSIE !!
KLAK
THIS IS WHERE WE PART WAYS.
VEGETA!!
ZOOM

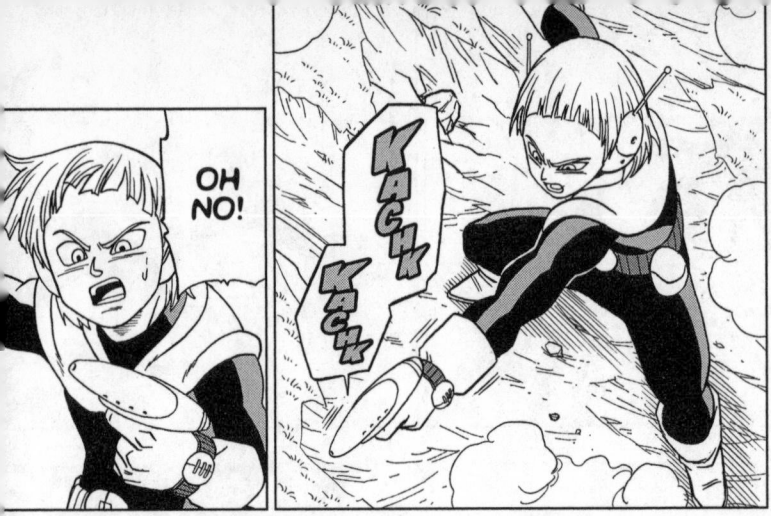
OH NO!
KACHK
KACHK

IT'S NOW OR NEVER, GOKU!!

SKF
SKF

BWAM

FWP
DAM-MIT!!
SLAM SLAM SLAM SLAM
!
WHERE'D THEY RUN OFF TO?!
THEY'RE GONE?
HUH?

OPEN UP.
ZOOM
GALACTIC PATROL HQ
BWUH?!
FSH

...
APOLOGIES FOR INTERRUPTING YOUR ROYAL BATH, GALACTIC KING!!
SORRY, MISTER. YOURS WAS THE ONLY CHI I COULD SENSE.
W-WHAT THE HECK?!
I DUNNO... WHAT COULD HE BE THINKING?
WHAT DO YOU THINK VEGETA MEANT BY ALL THAT?
DODGING ALL OUR SHOTS.
DAMMIT!
TCH!
PEW
PEW

THIS WILL GET BUMPY.
YOU MIGHT WANT TO GRAB HOLD OF SOME-THING.
BEEP BEEP
KACHIK
WOOM
KOOOM
W-WE LOST 'EM.
WHAT'RE YOU IDIOTS DOING?!

WE'RE HEADING BACK TO GALACTIC PATROL HQ TOO.
BEEP
BY THE SKIN OF OUR TEETH.
PHEW ...
WOOSH
FWIP
WE'RE GOING TO PLANET YARDRAT.
HUH?
W-WHERE'S THAT EXACTLY?
NO. YOU'RE GOING TO FLY THIS THING WHERE I WANT TO GO.

I'LL TELL YOU LATER.
WAIT. WHERE'S THAT?

CHAPTER 51: TO EACH THEIR OWN PLANS

FWSH FWSH FWSH
TMP
TMP TMP
W-WOW...
THE WHOLE PLANET DIED BEFORE WE KNEW IT!
VWOOM
PHEW...

LORD MORO, IT KINDA LOOKED LIKE THOSE GALACTIC PATROL GUYS JUST VANISHED.
THEY'VE GOTTA BE DEAD, RIGHT?
WITH THIS, MY PHYSICAL RECOVERY IS ES-SENTIALLY COM-PLETE.
PLANETS INHABITED SUCH UNIQ SPECIES POSSESS SPECTACL LAR ENERG
THERE ARE TWO AMONG THEM CAPABLEOF INSTANT TELE-PORTATION, INCLUDING THE GREAT LORD OF LORDS. THEY MUST HAVE ESCAPED AGAIN.
NO...
...SO I CHOOSE TO LET THEM ROAM THIS UNIVERSE LIKE LIVESTOCK. NATURALLY, I WILL KILL THEM SHOULD THEY INTERFERE AGAIN.
NEVER MIND THEM. INDIVIDUALS WITH THAT MUCH POWER ARE RARE ENOUGH...
WHICH GROUP SHOULD WE GO AFTER FIRST?
THEIR SPACE SHIP ALSO GOT AW
I'VE GOT SOME CHOICE PLANETS IN MIND.
OF COURSE. BEFORE WE GOT LOCKED UP BY THOSE GALACTIC LOSERS, MY CREW AND I RAMPAGED AROUND THIS WHOLE GALAXY...
IN THE MEANTIME, DO YOU KNOW OF ANY PLANETS WITH REMARKABLE LIFE FORCE? I WISH TO BUILD UP MY ENERGY RESERVES.

WHRRR
EXCELLENT. LEAD ME TO THEM.
AND I'LL SEND MY GUYS TO DO SOME SCOUTING. I'LL HAVE 'EM SEARCH EVERY NOOK AND CRANNY OF THE GALAXY.
WHRR
HUMMM
HUMMM
KLONK

ZOOSH
ZOOSH
WHRRRRL
FWIP
FWIP
WHRRRRL
FWP
KLAK

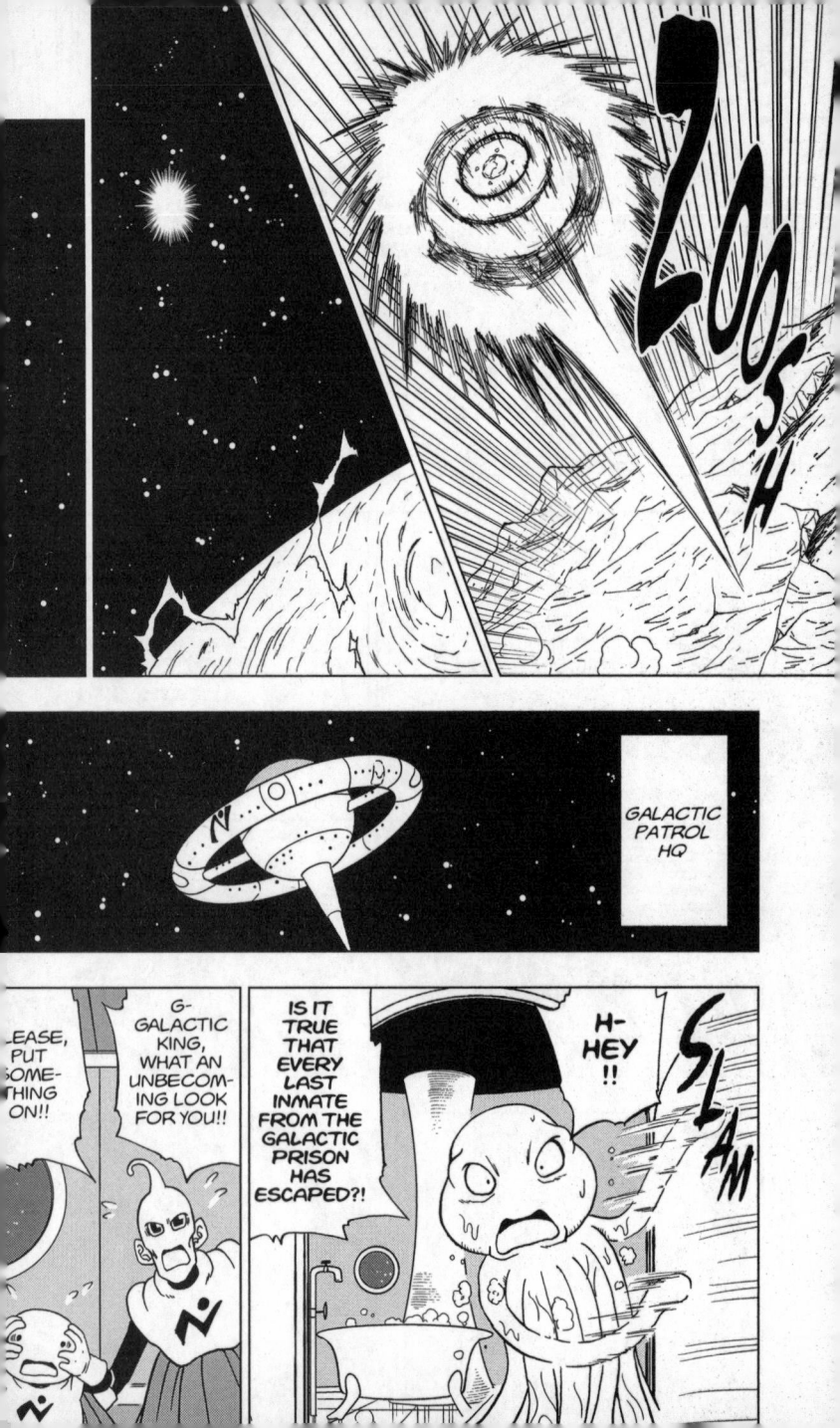
GOOSH
GALACTIC PATROL HQ
-EASE, PUT SOME-THING ON!!
G-GALACTIC KING, WHAT AN UNBECOM-ING LOOK FOR YOU!!
IS IT TRUE THAT EVERY LAST INMATE FROM THE GALACTIC PRISON HAS ESCAPED?!
H-HEY !!
SLAM

WHY WASN'T I TOLD?
I THOUGHT YOU KNEW, YOUR HIGHNESS...
H-HERE, YOUR ROYAL CROWN!
EEK!
PLOP
ARE YOU BLIND? HIS ROYALNESS HAS GOT HIS KINGLY CROWN ON!
ISN'T HE STILL NAKED?
WE HAD SOME OF OUR INTEL WIRES CROSSED HERE AT HQ.
I, UHHH...
HUH?
LET ME GUESS, YOU THINK I'VE BEEN WEARIN PANTS THIS WHOLE TIME?

YOU MEAN TO SAY THAT MORO AND THE ESCAPED CONVICTS REMAIN AT LARGE?
TALK ABOUT CULTURE SHOCK...
HUH?
I THOUGHT YOU WERE GOING TO SORT OUT THIS MESS, MERUS...
A-APOLOGIES, YOUR KINGLINESS !!
SHP SHP
...OUR MISSION ENDED IN TOTAL FAILURE!!
DESPITE THE PRESENCE OF AN ELITE SUCH AS MYSELF...
SO I'M AFRAID WE NEED TO RE-WORK OUR STRATEGY.
MORO GREW MORE POWERFUL THAN WE EXPECTED ...

GOKU!
DID BOO AND A LITTLE GREEN KID SHOW UP HERE EARLIER?
PSST! HEY.
ACTU-ALLY...
A CHILD
ZZZ
YOU'RE ALL RIGHT!
HEYA, ESCA!
I'M SO GLAD YOU WERE ABLE TO TELEPORT AWAY!
HMM? WHERE'S BOO?
YES.

UM, I DON'T SEE VEGETA WITH YOU.
BOO FOUGHT HARD OUT THERE FOR US. HE MUST BE WORN-OUT.
AFTER WE ARRIVED, HIS FACE CHANGED BACK AND HE FELL ASLEEP.
ZZZZ ZZZZ
I BET HE FLEW OFF TO TRAIN SOME-WHERE.
DON'T WORRY-- HE'S PROB-ABLY FINE.
WE CAN'T SIT ON OUR HANDS EITHER. ANYONE GOT A PLAN?
ONE THAT DOESN'T INVOLVE BOO?
ZZZZ ZZZZ
OUR NORMAL TACTICS DIDN'T WORK AGAINST MORO AT ALL, AND I'M THINKING THAT HIT VEGETA PRETTY HARD. HE MUST HAVE A NEW IDEA IN THE WORKS.
TO TRAIN, YOU SAY?

MORO DOESN'T SEEM TO BE PURSUING US. HE'S FLOWN OFF IN ANOTHER DIRECTION.
I CAN'T SENSE HIS CHI ANYMORE EITHER.
IT'S AS IF HE FLEW AWAY AT TOP SPEED.
THE GUY WHO WAS AT MORO'S SIDE.
HE'S THE LEADER OF A GANG OF BANDITS THAT ONCE RAMPAGED AROUND THE GALAXY.
SAGAN-BO?
...SO I CAN'T TRACK IT BY RADAR.
AUTOPILOT ACTIVATED.
SAGANBO'S SHIP IS THE FASTEST I'VE EVER KNOWN...
HIS STRENGTH MADE HIM TOUGH TO CAPTURE.
AH, THE ONE WHO DEALT A BLOW TO KAKARROT

OU'RE A FA-HER?
OH?
SO HAT IF I AM?
WITHOUT MORO AIDING HIM, EVEN MY BOY COULD DEFEAT HIM.
THAT FOOL WAS NO WORTHY OPPO-NENT.
AND NOW HE'S FREE AGAIN.
JUST UNEXPECTED. THAT'S ALL...
ERM...
SPEAKING IN TERMS OF YOUR EARTH TIME... ABOUT ONE WEEK.
NEVER MIND THAT. HOW MUCH FARTHER TO YARDRAT?
LET ME PLUG IN THE NUM-BERS ...
UM, VEGETA.
I'LL BE RESTING IN THE MEANTIME.
ALL RIGHT.

IT'S THE SAME TRIBE THAT TAUGHT KAKARROT INSTANT TELEPORTATION.
THE DENIZENS OF THAT PLANET AREN'T SUITED TO PHYSICAL COMBAT, BUT THEY EMPLOY A NUMBER OF STRANGE TECHNIQUES.
WHAT EXACTLY IS YOUR PLAN WHEN WE GET TO YARDRAT?
HMM?
PRECISELY.
SO YOU'RE HOPING THE YARDRATIANS KNOW A TRICK OR TWO THAT COULD HELP YOU HOLD YOUR OWN AGAINST MORO?
OH. I SEE
...
SLAM
KLK
THOUGH IT'S NOT STRATEG I RELISH

A FEW DAYS PASS IN THE GALAXY...
I WILL ACHIEVE VICTORY NEXT TIME.
OVER MORO, OVER THOSE CONVICTS...
I CAN'T AFFORD TO BE MADE A FOOL OF LIKE THAT AGAIN.
...AND OVER KAKARROT.

INTRODUCE YOURSELVES.
C'MON, BOYS.
BLAM BLAM BLAM BLAM BLAM
WHAT'S WITH THESE GUYS?!
GAH!
GUH... DAMMIT

PLANET ZOON
RMMMBL
W-WHATEVER HAPPENS, WE GOTTA PROTECT THE ROYAL TREASURE.
!
ZOOM
SHWP

THUD
ZRM
ACK...
GRAP
W-WHAT THE?!
MLEP
D-DAMM!!
LOOM

TMP
EEK!
KRAK
WHAK
WSH
SHWP
SHUNK
WSH
SLAM
SLAM

POP
SHWAP SHWAP
SPARKL
SPARKL
THIS SHOULD BE EVERYTHING WORTH ANYTHING ON THIS PLANET.
OH YEAH? GOOD WORK.
WE HIT THE JACKPOT, SAGANBO! THIS'S GOTTA BE WORTH A TON!
OOH!
GREAT! WE'RE PULLING OUT.

N-
NO,
WAIT.
ZAP
BOOM
GAHH!!

PYEW
BABABOOM
GAHHH!!
BA BA BOOM
GWAHH!!
THE MORE BODIES WE RACK UP, THE LESS ENERGY FOR LORD MORO TO SNACK ON.
CUT IT OUT, SEVEN THREE

TMP TMP

LET'S GO.
FWAH

SORRY ABOUT THE WAIT, LORD MORO.
WE'VE GOT ALL THE TREASURE FROM THIS PLANET.

SHOOM
SHOOM

WELL DONE.
AND NOW IT'S MEAL-TIME.

RMMMBL
GULP
NO MATTER HOW MANY PLANETS I WATCH DIE, IT STILL SENDS A CHILL DOWN MY SPINE.

HMM...
NOT A BAD PLANET.
THANK YOU.
VE SNAG THE OOT, AND YOU GET TO CHOW DOWN ON THE PLANET-- WE MAKE A PERFECT TEAM, HUH?
INDEED.
AND YOU WILL SURELY NEED RESOURCES OF VALUE ONCE MY DEALS ARE REALIZED.
SNAGGING VALUABLES IS OUR SPECIALTY, SO DON'T YOU WORRY.
BZZZT
WHAT IS IT?
INCOM-NG CALL FROM SOME OF OUR SCOUTS.

WHAK
WE FOUND A PLANET WITH SOME NICE ENERGY, I THINK.
SAGANBO!
BWOOM

SO IT'S OUR JOB TO STRIP THIS PLANET OF ITS TREASURES BEFORE THEY SHOW UP!

GWARR!
IT'S CRAWLING WITH ENERGETIC BEASTIES.

GREAT. WE'LL HEAD YOUR WAY.
AND WE'LL BE WAITING.
SHWP

THE WHOLE SQUAD'S COMING TO US, LADIES.
HEY.
THUD

THE 'ROBLEM S THEY'RE OVING AT UCH HIGH SPEEDS THAT 'VE KEEP LOSING THEM ON THE RADAR.
DID YOU MANAGE TO LOCK ONTO THEIR LIFE SIGNA-TURES?
THEY'VE PRO-GRESSED THAT FAR ALREADY?!
... PLANET ZOON HAS BEEN ANNIHI-LATED.
IT SEEMS...

...MORO HIMSELF HAS GOTTEN EVEN STRONGER.
AND AFTER A FEW DAYS OF THIS...
AND I CAN'T READ CHI SIGNA-TURES THAT FAR AWAY.
SO THA WON'T WORK.
I SUSPECT THAT MORO IS GOING AFTER PLANETS BEYOND OUR IMMEDIATE REACH...

DAMMIT... EVEN IF WE COULD CONFRONT MORO NOW... OUR ODDS OF VICTORY ARE VIRTUALLY ZERO.

EVEN IF **YOU** WERE FIGHTING SERIOUS-LY?

OF WHAT, EXACTLY?
MIND IF I RUN A LITTLE TEST?
HUH?
TWIT

WHE
SHU
HUH?
W-WHOA THERE GOKU!

THAT'S WHY I DODGED.
YES?
I THREW THAT PUNCH MEANING TO CONNECT.
DID AGENT MERUS SAY SOMETHING THAT MADE YA MAD?
I KNOW AGENT MERUS CAN BE A SNOBBISH, PRETENTIOUS, HEAVY-HANDED LEADER--I GET IT. BUT HE AIN'T ALL BAD.
WE'RE ALL FRIENDS HERE.
COME ON, GUYS.
I WANNA GET A FEEL FOR YOUR TRUE POWER, MERUS.
THE WAY THOSE BANGS ARE CHOPPED JUST A LITTLE TOO SHORT?
AND LOOK AT HIS FACE. IT'S KINDA ADORABLE, YEAH?

HMM?
I KNOW JUST THE PLACE.
VERY WELL.
SPAR WITH ME?
YOU GUYS EVEN GOT ONE OF THESE, HUH?
OOH...
...BUILT TO WITHSTAND A DECENT AMOUNT OF ABUSE.
THIS IS TRAININ ROOM JUST FOR US AGENTS ...

WELL... ON THAT NOTE...
...I'LL KICK THIS OFF.
BE MY QUEST.
IMP
FW
OOM
WHEF
SHO SHO SHO
WHEF WHEF WHEF

SHP
SINOOSH
TOMP
TMP
BWOOSH
SKF

FWP
TU
FWRL

KAR LL L
FLP
FLP
FLP
FLP
BWOOSH
TMP

FWAH
YOU
EOPLE
PEND
ME ON
HAT?
FIT-
NESS?
IN-
STEAD
OF
WASTING
TIME
WITH
THIS.
IS THAT ALL?
WE SHOULD
JUST SHOW HIM
THIS YEAR'S
PHYSICAL
FITNESS
RESULTS.
WHERE'S
THE BLOOD-
LUST?
GOKU
IS JUST
TESTING
MERUS'S
POWER.
WOW...
IF YOU'RE
CURIOUS,
I HOLD THE
TITLE FOR BEST
UPWARD-FACING
DOG POSE,
THREE YEARS
RUNNING.

SHWAH
WHF
SWP SWP SWP
HAHH!!
TMP
TMP
TCH!

KRK
KRK
OH NO !!
!
KRIK
KRAK
THIS PLACE CAN'T TAKE MUCH MORE!!
E-ENOUGH, GOKU!!

WHOOPS...
SORRY.
YOU'RE GONNA BRING THE ROO DOWN!!

OKAY, WE'RE DONE.

SHOOM

I THINK I'VE SEEN ENOUGH FOR NOW.
ARE YOU SATISFIED

HOW ABOUT YOU TRAIN ME?
I'VE GOT IT!
?
AND IT'S JUST LIKE I THOUGHT.
!
TRAIN-ING?
HMM? WHAT'D THAT CRAZY GOKU JUST SAY?
...IT SEEMS LIKE YOU KNOW PLENTY THAT I DON'T.
I STILL DON'T HAVE A TOTAL FEEL FOR YOUR STRENGTH, BUT...
AM I WRONG?

I'VE GOT A FEELING THAT TRAINING WITH YOU COULD GET ME CLOSER TO MASTERING IT.
IT'S ALL ABOUT LETTING THE BODY MOVE ON INSTINCT, SO IT MIGHT WORK AGAINST MORO EVEN WHEN HE STARTS ABSORBING MY ENERGY.
THERE'S A MOVE THAT I'M STILL TRYING TO MASTER.
GREAT!
I AM ALL TOO HAPPY TO ASSIST.
...
THEN THAT IS WHAT WE SHALL DO.
PHEW! CUZ IT IT'S NOT REAL TRAINING IF I CAN'T EVEN SWITCH TO GOD MODE.
BUT THIS ROOM CAN ONLY TAKE SO MUCH, SO I RECOMMEND ANOTHER LOCATION FOR YOUR TRAINING.

PLANET JUNG
HAND OVER ALL THE BLUE AURUM YOU FOLKS'VE PRO-CESSED.
THAT SAFE AIN'T GONNA OPEN ITSELF.
NOBODY'S SWOOPING IN TO SAVE THE DAY THIS TIME.
HA HA HA! TOO BAD FOR YOU, THE GALACTIC PATROL'S KINDA CLOSED FOR REPAIRS AT THE MOMENT.
W-WEREN'T YOU SCOUNDRELS ARRESTED BY THE GALACTIC PATROL?

LATER!
BANG
BANG
GA
YOU GOT IT!
CALL SAGAN-BO, GHETTI. GIVE HIM A GOOD STORY.
LUCKY BREAK FOR US, HUH? THE WHOLE GALAXY'S OURS FOR THE TAKING, AND AL IT TOOK WAS PRETENDING TO PLEDGE LOYALTY TO THAT MORO FELLA.
WHICH PLANET SHOULD WE PAY A VISIT TO NEXT?
BEEP
THIS PLANET WAS A BUST. NOT MUCH ENERGY, NO SIR. WE'RE OFF TO SEARCH FOR AN-OTHER.
CAPTAIN SAGAN-BO? THAT YOU?
WOOSH

WHAT'S THAT?
BRO, REMEMBER WHEN MERUS AND HIS MERRY GANG SHOWED UP TO HAUL US IN? I'M REMEMBERING SOMETHING THEY SAID.

THAT'S WHAT IT SOUNDED LIKE.
WELL, WELL... SO THIS EARTH PLACE HAS GOT ITS OWN STASH OF BLUE AURUM?
THAT PUNY AGENT OF THEIRS SAID THAT ON SOME PLANET CALLED EARTH, THEY CALL BLUE AURUM SKY-GOLD INSTEAD.
LET'S AMBLE ON OVER TO EARTH.
WELL WHAT'RE WE WAITING FOR?
YOU HEARD THEM FROM WAY UP THERE? KILLER PAIR OF EARS ON YOU, SIS.
WAKE UP, VEGETA! WE'VE ARRIVED!
AT THAT MOMENT, VEGETA FINALLY MADE IT TO YARDRAT...

DRAGON BALL SUPER

CHAPTER 52: GOKU AND VEGETA'S TRAINING

SO THESE ARE THE YARDRATIANS. I'VE NEVER ENCOUNTERED THEM BEFORE.
HEAR THEY OME IN ULTIPLE TYPES.

TMP TMP TMP

MOVE ASIDE, FOLKS.

TMP TMP TMP

WELCOME!
HOWDY!
YOU LOOK QUITE SIMPLE FOR A SAIYAN.
GRP
!
WE HEARD ALL ABOUT YOU FROM GOKU!
YOU MUST BE VEGETA
OH...
UH, THIS IS VEGETA

SHFFL SHFFL
YOU'RE ELCOME.
SO WE'RE ETERNALLY GRATEFUL TO YOU AND GOKU FOR TAKING CARE OF THAT PROBLEM.
I REMEMBER HEARING THEY'D ATTACKED THIS PLACE.
THE GINYU SQUAD CAUSED QUITE A STIR ON OUR PLANET BEFORE GOKU DEFEATED THEM.
YOU LOT?
OH.
HOOPS. SORRY.
WAS IT ONE OF YOU LOT?
WHO TAUGHT INSTANT TELEPOR-TATION TO KAKARROT?

HUH?
I'M HERE ON MY OWN.
...WAS ME.
THE ONE WHO TAUGHT GOKU INSTANT TELEPORTATION...
...
WHERE THEY AL GO?
WE'RE RATHER WEAK.
COPIES ?
COME ON IN AND MEET THE ELDER.
WHRRRR
SO SOMETIME WE MAKE COPIES O OURSELVE TO TRICK PEOPLE.

YOU LOOK QUITE SIMPLE FOR A SAIYAN.
AH, I'M NOT VEGETA. HE IS.
GRP
ALLOW ME TO INTRO-DUCE ELDER PYBARA.
YOU MUST BE VEGETA.
YES, SO DO YOU HAVE A TECHNIQUE TO MAKE THAT HAPPEN?
WELL, I THINK I UNDERSTAND. YOU'RE HOPING TO BEAT THIS MORO FELLOW.
WHAT?
WE ARE NOT BLESSED WITH SOME GREAT WEALTH OF TECH-NIQUES.
THERE'S BEEN A MISUNDER-STANDING, I'M AFRAID.

SPIRIT CON-TROL.
AND WHAT ONE THING IS THAT?
IT IS FROM THAT THAT ALL OUR ABILITIES ARE BORN.
WE DEVOTE OUR STUDIES TO ONLY ONE SINGLE THING.
YOU KNOW ABOUT IT?
WHAT WE CALL SPIRIT, GOKU CALLED CHI.
MEAN-ING?
FSH
FLK
INSTANT TELE-PORT-ATION...
BY THAT NAME, YES.
SHWP
SHWP
SHWP
SHWP
...MAKING COPIES...

HUH ...?
'HAT'S YOUR ORMAL SIZE?
FWOOMP
EVEN GIGANTI-FICATION.
VERY WELL.
STUDY HOW THE SPIRIT FUNCTIONS AND THE PATH WILL OPEN TO YOU AS WELL.
EVERYONE ON YARDRAT CAN DO THESE THINGS.
THESE ARE ACHIEVED BY SHIFTING, SPLITTING AND GROWING ONE'S VERY SPIRIT.
.THIS SO-CALLED SPIRIT CONTROL.
TEACH ME...

ROGER THAT! WE'LL HANDLE THINGS HERE.
I'LL BE AWAY FROM HQ FOR A BIT. CONTACT ME IF YOU NEED ANYTHING.
A FEW DAYS AFTER VEGETA LANDED ON YARDRAT, GOKU TRAVELED TO ANOTHER PLANET TO TRAIN WITH MERUS.
HMM...
WITH VEGETA MISSING AND GOKU TRAIN-ING WITH MERUS, WE'RE CLEARLY SHORT HANDED.
WE'RE IN NEED OF NEW RECRUITS, THEN...
WITH NO MAJOR CHANGES TO SPEAK OF, TIME PASSED UNPRODUCTIVELY AT HQ.
WE JUST DISPATCHED AGENTS TO PLANET RICCI. WE'RE RUNNING LOW ON PERSONNEL...
LOOKS LIKE THE CONVICTS SHOWED UP ON PLANET CHIP!
YOU MEAN PEOPLE WHO'D COME WILLINGLY, RIGHT?
Y-YEAH ...
HOW ABOUT THE SECTOR YO MANAGE, JACO?

AH!
WHAT?
OF COURSE! MONAKA!
WHAT ABOUT THAT OTHER WARRIOR FROM THE MATCH AGAINST UNIVERSE 6? WHERE IS HE? COULD WE SUMMON HIM HERE?
!
...
AMEK-
N, YOU SAY?
NO! I MEAN THE NAMEK-IAN.

THE SANCTUARY
...
THAT COULD BE IT, UN-LESS ...
OUR TELEPATHY DOES HAVE ITS LIMITS. THAT'S JUST HOW IT IS.
I CAN'T REACH ANYONE ON NEW NAMEK ...
NO GOO
IF NOTHING ELSE, I'M CERTAIN THAT SOMETHING TERRIBLE IS HAPPENING OUT IN SPACE.
...
...THE NAMEKIANS CAPABLE OF TELEPATHY ARE ALL DEAD.
HUH... Y-YOU DON'T MEAN ...?

ZOOM
LOOK THERE.
'HAT'S ARTH.
YOU SAID IT.
FIRST, LET'S FIND A PLACE TO LAND.
HERE'S HOPING IT'S GOT PLENTY OF BLUE AURUM.
PRETTY AS A PICTURE.

SOMEONE'S APPROACHING EARTH.
WHO...?
DO THEY HAVE SOMETHING TO DO WITH WHATEVER NASTY BUSINESS IS HAPPENING OUT IN THE GALAXY?
WHAT IS IT?
I'LL CHECK IT OUT.
ONE... TWO... THREE OF THEM?
I'M NO SURE
ZOOSH
NOT TO WORRY-- THEIR CHI SIGNATURES ARE WEAK.
BE CAREFU

ZOOM
WE CAN LAND AROUND HERE WITHOUT DRAWING ATTENTION.
GREAT. SET HER DOWN IN A GOOD SPOT.
HMM? SOME-ONE'S DOWN THERE.

YOU GOT IT.
GO ON-- BLAST HIM TO BITS.
TCH... WHAT A PAIN.
MAYBE HE SAW US FLYING IN FROM SPACE?
WHAT DOES HE WANT?
KACHK
POP
BLAM
BLAM
BLAM
BLAM

BOOM BOOM BOOM
SHARP SHOOT-ING.
RMMMBL
WOOSH
WOOOSH

UP THERE!
ABOVE US!!
WHAT ?
WHERE'D HE GO?
BRO! HE'S GONE!!
HRM?
...IS THIS GUY?
WH-WHO THE HECK...
TERRIBLE MANNERS FOR A GUEST.
SHOOTING FIRST WITHOUT ASKING QUESTIONS

VWOOM
THEY CERTAINLY DON'T SEEM LIKE BIG THREATS.
BULMA!
DENDE, HOW'S IT GOING?
IS PICCOLO AROUND?
WHAT BRINGS YOU HERE?

WE JUST GOT WORD FROM JACO.
CAN I HELP YOU?
HE JUST LEFT.
PICCC LO?
HE'S COMING HERE TO DRAFT PICCOLO INTO THE GALACTIC PATROL.
C.CORP
...JACO DIRECT-LY?
...WHY DON'T WE ASK...
IS THE GALACTIC PATROL BATTLING SOMEONE OR SOMETHING AT THE MOMENT?
HUH
PLEASE TELL ME EVERYTHING YOU KNOW.
I DON'T HAVE THE DETAILS, BUT...

SHOOM
SKF
SKF
GAH !!
FRAK

TUG
TCH
FLIK
FLIK
FSH
FSH
FWP
FWAH
FWAH
FWP
FWP
FWP
FWAH

BWAH
THMP
THMP
THMP
BOOM
BOOM
BOOM
BOOM
BOOM
SNAP
FWAHH

YABOOM
DASH

ORMP
POOF
PWOOF
TUG
GOT HIM!!
GRAP

HUH?
!
BOOF
BOOF
GRAP
GRAP
KYAH!
GWAH!

TOO BAD FOR YOU, I'M MORE THAN USED TO THAT MOVE.
WHAP
WHAP
G- GET OFFA ME!!
GAHHH!!
FWIP

SLAM
FLING
!
YEOWCH...
RGH...
W-WHAT'S WITH THIS PLANET?
HOW'D IT COME TO BE HOME TO A POWERFUL BEING LIKE THIS?
THUD

O-OH NO.
HOW WFUL.
AND THAT SAME TRAGEDY'S PLAYING OUT OVER AND OVER ACROSS THE GALAXY.
GET IT? NAMEK IS A DEAD PLANET NOW...
I'M HEADING YOUR WAY, SO GATHER THEM UP, OKAY?
MAYBE ALSO SON GOKU'S SON, OR THOSE BALDIES?
AND SINCE VEGETA AND GOKU ARE OFF TRAINING, YOU'RE COMING TO PICCOLO FOR HELP?
MY FELLOW NAMEK-IANS...
DARN RIGHT.
YOU EARTHLINGS MAY BE TOTAL WIMPY WEAKLINGS, BUT ALL THOSE LIFE-FORMS YOU'VE GOT WOULD MAKE YOUR PLANET A TANTALIZING TREAT FOR MORO. HE'LL GOBBLE THE PLACE UP ONCE HE FINDS OUT.
PLANETS FOR MORO TO EAT.
AND BE ON ALERT! MORO SENT A BUNCH OF SCOUTS OUT INTO THE GALAXY.
KURIRIN AND TEN-SHINHAN? YOU GOT IT.
WHAT'RE THEY LOOKING FOR?
OH YEAH?

HMM? UM... THEY'D COME IN GROUPS OF TWO OR THREE IN A LONG, THIN SPACESHIP.
HOW WOULD WE RECOGNIZE THESE SCOUTS?
OH NO, WHAT IF...
!
IT CAN'T BE...
IT...
ARE YOU CONNECTED TO WHATEVER IS HAPPENING OUT IN SPACE?
WHO ARE YOU?
DAM MIT

SORRY FOR BEING SO QUICK ON THE DRAW. THAT'S ON US.
...
WE'RE JUST YOUR FRIENDLY NEIGH-BORHOOD ALIENS, PASSING THROUGH.
WHAT ARE YOU TALKING ABOUT?
WE WON'T BOTHER YOU NONE, SO PLEASE LET US GO, OKAY?
SMART THINKING AS ALWAYS, BRO!
THAT'LL BE OUR CHANCE TO MAKE OFF WITH THE BLUE AURUM.
MORO'LL BE ITCHING TO TAKE THIS PLANET ONCE WE SEND WORD.
WE'RE REALLY JUST GONNA SLINK OFF?

FLIK
WE SURE AIN'T.
IT'S CLEAR YOU THREE AREN'T THE SOURCE OF THE GREATER DISTURBANCE.
!
SHLUFF
FWOOM
AND NEVER COME BACK.
GO ON.
MUCH APPRECIATED, GREEN FELLA.

ZOOM
DON'T LET THEM GET AWAY, PICCOLO!!
W-WAIT, NO.
HMM? SOMETHING'S FLYING AWAY.
!

THEY'RE ALLIED WITH THE GANG CAUSING TROUBLE OUT IN SPACE!
WHAT?
DENDE ?!
VWOOOM
NO THANK YOU.
WE'D BETTER HURRY.
SOME-ONE ELSE?
KAZOOSH

TCH!
BWAM
BOOM
GAHHH !!
ZOOM
KRASH
UGH ...

IT'S ONLY A MATTER OF TIME BEFORE THE CONVICTS PAY THIS ROCK A VISIT.
HEH HEH... YOU'RE TOO LATE. WE JUST SENT WORD TO THE MAIN FORCES.
YOU TRIED TO TRICK ME, HUH?
TMP
HA HA HA HA HA HA HA HA HA HA HA HA...
AND A NICE PLANET LIKE THIS? MORO'LL GULP IT DOWN BEFORE YOU KNOW WHAT HIT YOU.
CON-VICTS?
SERVE YOU RIGHT

ZOOSH
IF THEY AVE BEEN ILLED, THE PLANET THEY FOUND MUST BE HOST TO STRONG BEINGS INDEED.
HMM ...
I GUESS SO.
IT'S VORTH ERIFY-ING.
WHAT DO WE DO, LORD MORO?
INCOMING MESSAGE FROM THE MACARENI GANG. THEY SAID, "HELP US," THEN GOT CUT OFF.
WHAT NOW, SAGANBO?
IF IT PROVES TO BE A QUALITY PLANET, I WILL DEVOUR IT MYSELF.
SEND A STRONGER SCOUTING PARTY.

AS THE FORCES OF DARKNESS ENCROACH UPON THE EARTH, GOKU AND MERUS BEGIN TRAINING...
YAH!
KLAT KLAT
HAH! HAH!
KLAT KLAT KLAT KLAT
FWP FWP FWP
KLAT KLAT KLAT
FWP FWP FWP FWP

FWSH
FWP
TMP
GAH!!
WHAK
SHOOM

SHP
SKF SKF SKF
WHIRL
NO, IT'S NOT QUITE THAT SIMPLE.
I'M JUST NOT GETTING IT.
I GOTTA EMPTY MY HEART AND MIND FOR THAT MOVE TO WORK, BUT WHEN I'M FIGHTING, MY EMOTIONS ARE ALL OVER THE PLACE.
DARN... IT'S NOT WORKING.
DASH

FWP FWP FWP
RAGE, GRIEF, JOY-- THOSE STRONG EMOTIONS CAN TRANSLATE TO PRODIGIOUS POWER.
THAT ONE'S TRIGGERED BY RAGE.
YEAH.
JUST LIKE YOUR SUPER SAIYAN TRANS-FORMATION.
BUT THE TECHNIQUE YOU'RE AFTER IS THE OPPOSITE.

!
TMP
FWSH
TMP
TMP
TOMP
WHAP

SUCH IS ULTRA INSTINCT.
...IN THE FACE OF A JARRING SHOCK TO YOUR EMOTIONS.
IT WILL ACTIVATE WHEN YOU ACHIEVE SELF-CONTROL...
NO NEED TO BE SORRY.
'M SURE OU HAD A REASON.
YES...
YES.
YOU KNEW ABOUT IT ALL ALONG?
SHING
BEEP
I APOLOGIZE FOR KEEPING THIS FROM YOU.

I ALREADY KNOW YOU'RE A GOOD GUY AND YOU WANNA BEAT MORO AS BAD AS ME, YEAH? THAT'S GOOD ENOUGH FOR ME.
TOTALLY FINE-- SAY NO MORE.
WE DON'T HAVE ALL THE TIME IN THE WORLD.
SO FORGET ALL THAT, AND LET'S GET BACK TO TRAIN-ING.
FOLLOW ME, GOKU.
ANY DOUBTS I HAD ARE GONE NOW.
VERY WELL
KREEK
WHAT THE ...?

YOUR TRAINING WILL CONTINUE IN HERE.
!
SLAM
EVERY DAY THAT PASSES IN THE OUTSIDE WORLD GIVES US THREE DAYS IN HERE.
SO YOU'RE FAMILIAR THEN?
THE CHAMBER OF SPIRIT AND TIME, RIGHT?
OH, I KNOW ALL ABOUT THIS PLACE.
BECAUSE I CAN UNLEASH MY FULL POWER WITHOUT ANYONE FINDING OUT.
?
WHILE THE TIME DILATION IS HELPFUL, WHAT'S MOST IMPORTANT IS THAT THIS SPACE IS SEALED OFF FROM THE WORLD.
ONLY THREE DAYS? I GUESS EVEN A LITTLE EXTRA TIME IS BETTER THAN NONE.

TO BE CONTINUED!

OH? CAN ARDLY IM-GINE.
AND THEN, ANOTHER SAIYAN SHOWED UP, BUT GET THIS-- HE WAS WAY STRONGER THAN US.
GALACTIC PATROL HQ: GOKU SUMMARIZED RECENT EVENTS ON EARTH FOR MERUS.
SPECIAL COMIC
FREEZA CAME TO EARTH OOKING FOR HE DRAGON BALLS, AND IE BROUGHT BROLY WITH HIM.
YEAH. HIS NAME IS BROLY.
HE KEPT GETTING STRONGER AND STRONGER AS WE FOUGHT, UNTIL HE FINALLY TURNED INTO A SUPER SAIYAN.
ONCE HE TRANSFORMED, WE COULDN'T EVEN BEAT HIM IN OUR SUPER SAIYAN BLUE FORMS, SO ME AND VEGETA HAD TO PERFORM FUSION.

SOME-HOW, WE WON.
HOW DID HE END UP THERE?
VAMPA?! THIS FELLOW LIVES IN SUCH A HOSTILE ENVIRON-MENT?!
TO A PLANE-TOID CALLED VAMPA.
I DON'T THINK HE WAS ACTUALLY A BAD GUY... ANYWAY, HE WENT BACK HOME.
W-WAIT! WHERE'S HE NOW? WHAT IF DECIDES TO COME BACK FOR MORE...?
I FOR-GET.
DUNNO. DO YOU REMEM-BER, VEGETA?
NO... I FEEL AS THOUGH THIS MUST BE MY FATHER'S FAULT, SOME-HOW...
MAYBE HE JUST LIKES LIVING IN SUCH A NASTY PLACE. WHAT A WEIRDO.
THESE TWO COULDN'T HAVE KNOWN ABOUT THE GRAND TALE WEAVED BY THEIR PARENTS' GENERATION...
(ORIGINALLY APPEARED IN JUMP VICTORY CARNIVAL 2019 OFFICIAL GUIDEBOOK)

YOU'RE READING THE WRONG WAY!

Dragon Ball Super reads from right to left, starting in the upper-right corner. Japanese is read from right to left, meaning that action, sound effects, and word-balloon order are completely reversed from English order.